THE STEWARDESS'S DIARY - PART TWO

MEXICO

S.M. PRATT

The Stewardess's Diary - Part Two: Mexico
Copyright © 2015 by S.M. Pratt

Last updated January 25, 2020
Editing by Samantha Marie

ISBN: 978-0-9940630-5-2 (e-book)

ISBN: 978-1-988639-21-5 (paperback)

PROLOGUE

I'M CHARLIE, a veteran pilot for a major international airline that shall remain nameless for reasons you'll soon come to understand.

A year ago, while waiting for my flight to London in the airline's lounge at one of America's largest hubs, I discovered a special and highly personal journal among my belongings. How it happened, I'll never know, but the beautiful brown leather notebook nonetheless appeared in my briefcase at some point between the time I left my New York penthouse apartment and arrived at the airport lounge.

Perhaps it was a mix-up at security, or some devious stewardess with sly hand skills, but I've since become obsessed with the person who wrote that diary, her stories, and—to be blunt—her unconventional sex life.

My best friend—let's call him Bob—is one of my regular co-pilots. Bob advised me to forget about the journal and ignore my hunch to track down its rightful owner. After my initial reading of her hand-written accounts, the part of me who's loyal to the airline and wants the best for our passengers certainly needed to find that stewardess and expel her from our company—or whatever airline she's with. This woman is surely a threat to any crew with her irreverent disregard for our uniforms, her sexual behavior with passengers and airline employees, and the way she ignores regulations. She should clearly be punished for her conduct...

But after reading and re-reading each one of her journal entries, another, more animal part of me has grown fond of her complete lack of boundaries, her willingness to experiment, and her ravenous sexual appetite.

I've had my fair share of illicit affairs with female flight attendants and co-pilots, but none of them were interesting enough to be granted a second fuck by yours truly, let alone be courted or considered for a long-term relationship. But the woman who's filled so many pages with delicate calligraphy and salacious words deserves my full attention. She's certainly maintained it well past the time I closed the cover of her journal—again and again.

Imagining how her naiveté was gradually—and most willingly—robbed from her was simply... enthralling. She's been haunting my wet dreams.

Now, every time I see an unknown stewardess, I wonder if *she*'s the one.

After many conversations with Bob over the past months during our overseas flights, I've come to share some of her journal entries with him. He agrees that I need to locate her. If not for the airline's sake or to satisfy my personal curiosity, then for the mere reason that I could stop obsessing about her and resume paying attention to my actual job: piloting giant aircrafts and safely getting passengers from point A to point B.

The following short stories record my obsession toward her. There are ten in total. Each installment contains my mystery stewardess's original journal entries for a specific location, followed by my own experiences in trying to track her down. You'll discover what (and whom) I did in an effort to identify and locate my stewardess based on the clues she's left in her diary. You can read the episodes in any order, but they'll probably make more sense if you start from the beginning and follow along as I attempt to find her.

And, just to be clear, these stories should *not* land in the hands of any prude or underage person. Some are just romantic, sensual, or highly erotic, while others are immoral, perverse, and possibly even illegal in some parts of the world.

Ah, the things I'll do to this mystery stewardess when I finally encounter her in the flesh!

I'm hard just thinking about it...

Yours truly,
Capt. Charlie

Undisclosed Airline

PART ONE

THE STEWARDESS'S ENTRIES

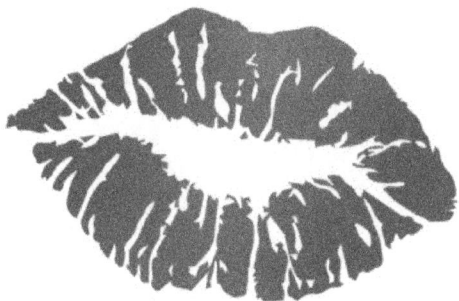

CONFIRMED passenger list printed and walkie-talkie in hand, I stood by the glass door a few feet away from the counter, waiting for the crew to report that our Cancun-bound plane was ready for boarding.

Can't wait to get there.

Kate and I had spent the past thirty minutes at the gate, reassuring an incessant stream of pasty-white passengers concerned about possible delays.

Don't think I'm the only one who's anxious to get my feet in the sand and body under the hot sun.

But my plans for this three-day-weekend included a few more extra-curricular activities with Matt—my friend with benefits. Lazy mornings, sex, brunch, swimming... Did I mention lots of sex? Or *good rolls in the sack* as he calls them...

Gosh, I can't believe it's already been a month since we met, during his very short stint as a flight attendant.

We shared a few pleasant evenings here and there, mostly when our schedules happened to coincide. Nothing serious, conversation over wine and cheese, and lots of hot sex.

He's soooo frigging handsome.

And I'd managed to keep thinking of him as something other than boyfriend material. Not quite the string of one-night stands my friend Alex had recommended, but still...

I'd made progress. My disillusion about *finding the one* was hibernating. My sexual life was headed in the right direction.

Hanging out with Matt for three delicious long nights and two full days would be so nice. I missed his hands on my body, his tongue on my—

My cellphone vibrated in my pocket, interrupting my daydream.

I dug it out, and the small pop-up showed I'd received a text message from Matt.

With butterflies in my stomach and a big grin on my face, I swiped my way past the password protection screen to read his words:

Sorry

Have to cancel weekend plans

Back with ex

Will explain later

Sorry, babe :(

12:20 P.M.

WHAT THE FUCK?

Ten minutes to boarding. And *now* I learned I was about to spend three days alone in a party town during the busy season *without* a hotel reservation... or any plans, really.

Shit.

What can I reply to that?

I shook my head for a few seconds, letting all the things I really wanted to say escape my mind, then I settled on sending the plain and politically-correct "ok."

I returned my phone to my jacket pocket, trying to don a happy face and push my anger and worries down my throat. The walkie-talkie finally screeched the report I'd been waiting for, so I acknowledged it and then returned to Kate at the counter.

I placed a hand on her elbow. "Time to make the announcement," I told her.

She nodded, flipped her brown hair behind her ear, and then picked up the handset.

While listening to her read the pre-written script in English then in Spanish to announce we'd soon start boarding families with young children and those who needed special assistance, I glanced at the crowd. A couple of families were getting their things together and coming our way. I didn't have much time, but maybe Kate could help.

When she hung up, I used the couple of minutes we still had to talk to her. I knew it would become impossible once the actual boarding process began.

"Kate, are you staying in Cancun?"

She shook her head. "No, I'm deadheading to San Francisco a couple of hours after we land. Are you?"

"I was planning to, but my... *friend* canceled on me." It still felt funny whenever I had to refer to him. He wasn't my *boyfriend*. *Fuck-buddy* just seemed flat-out rude, and I wasn't sure if *fucker* would have been a better label right now.

Then again, Matt didn't owe me anything. I couldn't be mad at him for canceling on me.

But it still sucked.

Her answer brought me back to reality. "That's too bad, but I'm sure you'll have fun anyway. Weather's supposed to be great!"

She started walking, covering the few feet that separated the counter from where she'd be checking our passengers' tickets.

"Do you have friends in Cancun?" I asked. "Someone who may have a couch or bedroom where I could crash?"

"No. Why do you ask? Don't you have a reservation?"

"No, unfortunately."

Her mouth made an upside-down U and she raised her eyebrows. "Good luck with that. Hotels near the beach are gonna be packed. You'll pay through the nose... if you find something!"

I'll be fine. I'll figure something out, I told myself while smiling at the tired-looking father of three standing in front of me with his offspring. I greeted him and took the boarding passes he was handing me.

1:20 P.M.

A HANDFUL of straggling and slightly inebriated last-minute passengers having joined us, we finally closed the gate.

Kate and I quickly walked around economy class, closing all overhead bins and ensuring our complete planeload of excited passengers was accounted for and seated in a full upright position, with their seat belts on. As ordered by the captain, we put the doors on automatic, cross-checked them, and then reported back.

Once we pushed away from the gate, the safety video started airing.

I love these modern planes with individual monitors that take away the need for our in-person safety demonstrations.

Only ten percent of passengers paid attention to those anyway. I don't know if more people are watching the video, but I hope so.

I headed to my seat, which faced the front row in economy class. It was the most socially-awkward seat in the plane.

Most passengers probably feel like I'm just staring at them, especially those trying to make a quick call after we make it clear their phones have to be put on airplane mode.

I decided to smile my way through the uncomfortable minutes spent facing the passengers.

Won't be long until I can get up again.

Let's see, maybe I know someone on this flight. Someone I can hang out with this weekend...

NO, I don't know anyone. Damn it.

The intercom crackled overhead. "Hi there, folks. Captain speaking. Due to a fairly long line of planes taxiing to take off on the runway in front of us, we expect a slight delay. We're... seventh in line. Please sit tight, keep your seat belt on, and refrain from using the washroom. We should be leaving the tarmac in about ten minutes. Thanks for your patience and sorry for the delay."

Oh goody.

MY CHEEKS WERE GETTING a little sore from fake-smiling and I'd run out of things and people to look at without staring. I obviously couldn't check my phone while facing everyone; that'd be a sure way to get our passengers upset.

Instead, I opted to start listening in to the conversation people sitting directly in front of me, close to the window, were having. Two beautiful, twenty-something blondes with perfect tans, long legs, and barely any clothes on were chatting and giggling. Next to them, in the aisle seat, a thirty-something, rugged, muscular Latino man with a crew cut introduced himself to the blonde sitting closest to him.

Military? Police?

The man who'd called himself Sebastian spoke English with a Spanish accent.

The ponytailed woman sitting next to him in the middle seat introduced herself as Isabel, then turned her attention back to her wavy-haired friend sitting by the window.

"Tracy, you'll love the birthday present I got you," Isabel said.

"You got me something? You didn't have to, Sweetie," the woman in the mini-skirt replied before kissing her friend on the lips.

Ah, they're together. Good for them.

...And less competition for the rest of us, plain-looking, mere-mortal, older straight women.

Tracy, the birthday girl sitting by the window, turned to her girlfriend to whisper something in her ear. I didn't want to make it obvious I had been listening, so I looked down. However, my eyes stopped on their path when I saw that, in leaning toward her girlfriend, the birthday girl had parted her knees by about a foot and, with her mini-skirt being so short, I currently had full-frontal view of her blonde pussy.

Trying not to react or stare was hard.

I've looked too long already.

17

I glanced up again. The birthday girl had moved her attention to me, and she sent a slight smile and a wink my way.

Blood rushed to my cheeks.

Totally not appropriate! Need to think about something else, fast. Small talk.

"So, where are you all going? Home?" I asked, mostly directing my question at Sebastian to avoid the women's stares.

"Back to work for me," he said.

"What kind of work do you do?" I continued, pleased to have succeeded in my attempt at distraction.

"Search and rescue, but I mainly patrol the coast on a boat."

"Neat. Must be nice to spend time on the water instead of in the air!" I replied.

"We love spending time on the water, too," Tracy, the pussy-exhibitionist, started before placing her hand on her girlfriend's lap. "Isn't that the best thing in the world, Isa?"

"Love it. My family has a nice yacht that we take out. This weekend, it'll just be the two of us, to celebrate Tracy's birthday."

Isabel had a melodious voice. She smiled at the coastguard, myself, and then her girlfriend while she replied, then she squeezed Tracy's knee, moving it once more to expose her girlfriend's pussy.

I swallowed hard. *I've stared at it twice now. Get a grip, girl!*

I wasn't playing for that team, but somehow I couldn't help looking.

Curiosity? Probably.

Both women were now grinning at me. They were obviously doing it on purpose.

What did they whisper to each other earlier?

"Tracy and Isabel," the coastguard started before his face turned stern. "Be careful out there. We've recently had reports of a few pirates boarding unsuspected sailors and stealing their boats."

"Pirates? Like Johnny Depp? You've gotta be kidding." The two blondes giggled.

"I wish I was. But I'm serious. Don't go too far off the coast without other boats around you."

Isabel was shaking her head. "Really? Nah."

"This *is* important, girls. I'm not joking." He shifted on his seat and grabbed the wallet from his cargo pant pocket. He opened it and dug a business card out of it, which he then handed to Isabel. "Here's my number. If you intend on sailing out alone, keep contact with me via text messages and send me your location."

Isabel took his card and thanked him. "Maybe you can come over for dessert if you're in the area," she offered with her velvety voice.

Maybe it was her friend's exposed pussy that had my mind down the gutter, but I'm pretty sure Isabel was flirting with Sebastian.

"That could be interesting. You girls like to party a lot?"

I'm not crazy. He got the same vibe.

The loud roar of the airplane's turbines suddenly filled the air. The passengers sunk in their seats while I purposely pushed my back into mine, trying to compensate for the inertia and acceleration that wanted to throw me face first toward the back.

We were powering up and taking off, finally.

4:55 P.M.

I SPENT the entire flight on my feet, attending to hungry and excited passengers who didn't want to waste a second of their vacations. The lesbian couple in the front row, along with most of the young adults flying in economy class, were partaking in a fair amount of onboard drinking. Overpriced beers were a hot commodity.

Each time I answered one of the blondes' service calls, they greeted me with large grins. They even tried to tip me on their sparkling wine purchases, but I couldn't accept.

"Why don't you get yourself a drink then? On us?" Isabel suggested.

I thought about it for a second. *It's against regulations, but who'd know?*

"Sure, why not? I'd like one of those mini wine bottles to wind down after work. Thanks, ladies," I said handing them each their unopened mini-bottles that Isabel had just purchased. I made a mental note to sneak one of those tasty—and now paid-for—bottles into my purse before leaving the aircraft in an hour or so.

The coastguard was drinking beer, keeping up with the party girls next to him with his eyes blatantly surveying Isabel's cleavage.

"And you, would you like another one?" I asked him.

His eyes glanced away from Isabel's breasts and met mine. He ordered another beer and reached for his wallet. I entered the transaction in the payment processing device while he was pulling out his card.

As I reached out to take his Visa, unexpected turbulence sent me crashing into him. Like the arm of a mother instinctually reaching out to protect a child sitting in the passenger seat of a car, Isabel's arms instantly stretched out to protect both Tracy and Sebastian. But her hand—conveniently?—cupped my left breast in the process. She nonetheless prevented my shoulder from landing square in Sebastian's jaw, and I was grateful for that.

Frantic commotion echoed all around us in the plane, followed by an announcement from the captain: "Sorry about that little bump, folks. Looks like we'll be flying through a small turbulent area for a few more minutes. Please return to your seats and fasten your seat belts."

Isabel winked at me, gave my breast a gentle squeeze, and then lowered her arm back to her lap. Tracy bent down to grab the sparkling wine bottles that had rolled onto the floor, thankfully still unopened. I apologized to Sebastian, but he would hear nothing of it.

"Maybe you need to get your feet on a boat for a change," Tracy suggested. "What do you think, babe?" she asked her girlfriend.

Isabel nodded. "That's a great idea. Are you staying in Cancun for a few days, or are you taking off to another exciting destination right away?"

"I'm sticking around for the weekend," I replied, finally feeling hopeful that I may have found some people to hang out with.

"Would you like to join us?" Tracy asked.

I looked at Tracy, then Isabel. Both had genuine smiles on. *What else am I going to do? Could be good fun:*

beautiful women, a boat, the ocean, drinks, maybe the handsome coastguard would be invited too?

"Sure, why not?" I said.

"Wonderful. You'll sit here again during landing?" Isabel asked, pointing at the vacant seat facing them.

"Yep," I said, nodding. "Best seat in the house." The words left my mouth without thinking, out of habit as it had become a running joke among my flight attendant friends. None of us liked sitting in front of the passengers, facing them. Isabel's eyes illuminated, and both she and her girlfriend burst out giggling.

I could once again feel blood rushing to my face. "If you'll excuse me, I have to continue my garbage run. We'll chat later," I said before pushing my cart down the aisle and collecting an empty water bottle from the young woman sitting behind them.

I RETURNED to my front-row seat after checking that all passengers' belongings had been properly stowed, seats in their upright positions, and seat belts fastened. The blondes and the coastguard were pretty happily drunk by now, and several passengers had their passports in hand, custom forms filled out and at the ready. A few were fidgeting, but most had a big smile on their faces.

After fastening my own seat belt, I noticed that Tracy and Isabel had traded seats. Tracy, the birthday girl, now sat next to Sebastian, her lap covered by a sweatshirt. *Good! Won't be caught inadvertently staring at her naked pussy one more time.*

A beep echoed in the main cabin, preceding the

captain's final announcement. "We're now approaching our final descent. We should be at the gate in about five minutes." While he continued with the standard *thank-you-for-choosing-us* bit, Sebastian leaned in to Tracy and then whispered something in her ear. I took another glance at the other rows. Many passengers were looking into the closest portholes to see the ocean and coast below, alternating between the port and starboard sides depending on which way the plane was leaning.

When the plane started veering to starboard again, bringing clouds into view on our side of the plane, the passengers' stares went to the portholes on the opposite side.

I saw Isabel slide her hand under the sweatshirt that rested on her girlfriend's lap.

A second later, a grin appeared on Tracy's face. Sebastian was still whispering sweet nothings into Tracy's ear, none the wiser.

Probably too tipsy to notice.

I felt Isabel's stare and turned to look at her. She smiled at me before speaking. "I'm sure we'll have a lot of fun this weekend when you join us on the boat."

Tracy giggled and sent a furtive glance my way

before returning her attention to Sebastian. A couple of minutes later, Tracy's hand launched toward Isabel, grabbing her firmly by the knee. Tracy then turned to stare at me, biting her lip, her eyes starting to go up in a pre-orgasmic stare, but she closed them again, her cheeks brightening, her chest raising higher—lifting her cropped top higher and exposing more of her flat stomach. Then, a few seconds later, Tracy let out a loud sigh, turned to face Isabel, and then kissed her.

"Thank you, baby. I needed that," she said to her girlfriend. Their eyes stayed locked for a few more seconds, and then they both turned and smiled at me. I swallowed hard. I felt the heat on my cheeks, but I had nowhere I could flee to. I was stuck in my discomfort zone between voyeurism and guilt.

The aircraft's wheels hit the tarmac, creating a vibration that reverberated through the cabin, and the plane steadied its course after dealing with a split second of cross-wind on the landing strip. Some of the passengers clapped. Sebastian crossed himself. *Superstitious or religious?* Either way, I was certainly happy that today's oddly sensual work shift was nearly over.

"So, you'll meet us at *La Esperanza Marina*

around 10 a.m. tomorrow morning?" Tracy asked, her cheeks flushed.

I nodded. I hadn't been on a boat in so long, and it definitely hadn't been part of my original weekend plans, but I had no doubt it would be filled with surprises.

"Should I bring anything?" I asked.

Isabel shook her head. "Your bikini... or nothing really. We've got everything we need. Look for *Delicious Sunset*. We'll be expecting you."

MY OVER-WORRYING about not finding a hotel room turned out to have been pointless.

I managed to find a comfortable room in a hotel close to the airport. Sure, it wasn't the Ritz-Carlton and it wasn't on the beach, but at least it was a place to leave my belongings, kick off my shoes, and crack open that tiny sparkling wine bottle.

I opened the patio door and let the warm tropical air into my room. Songs of piña coladas and sailing with Captain Morgan echoed in my mind as I leaned on the guard rail, watching the last pink and orange hues color the evening sky while sipping the now barely-cool, bubbly liquid.

Tomorrow should be interesting.

I FOUND the *Delicious Sunset* without problems. It was one of the nicest yachts at *La Esperanza*, and everyone around seemed to know the two luscious blondes.

After I crossed the small walkway to step onboard, Tracy welcomed me wearing the tiniest of bikinis and a matching hot pink hair clip in her shoulder-length, wavy hair. 'Weirdly-knotted-strings-with-three-tiny-triangles-of-hot-pink-fabric' would have been a better name for her outfit, but she pulled it off. At least her pussy was covered with one of those triangles. That was already a big change from her airplane apparel.

"Isabel, our guest is here," she yelled out after hugging me for a solid ten seconds.

Her girlfriend came up from below deck wearing a similar bikini, except that hers was white. Just like Tracy's, her entire body was tanned—with the possible exception of what the three tiny triangles covered, but I highly doubted it. Women with such bodies and access to a boat had all the reasons in the world to bare it all and get a full-body tan.

Tracy grabbed my overnight bag and headed to wherever her girlfriend had come from.

Isabel walked toward me, arms open and at the ready for a hug. We embraced. After a few seconds, she pulled away from me, her hands on my elbows and a large smile on her freckled face. "Come on, I'll give you the grand tour," Isabel said, grabbing my hand and pulling me. Then she suddenly stopped, turned, and took a second glance at me, my light-blue summer dress seemingly the cause of her concerns. "You brought a bikini, right?"

"I've got a swimsuit and towel in my bag," I replied, pointing in the direction Tracy had disappeared with my belongings.

She nodded and then began her quick tour of

the upper deck. The stern featured a nice patio-like space with cushions lining the U-shaped sitting area, a table, and large speakers attached to the bulkhead. Ten to twelve people could comfortably sit there and party all day.

We then headed toward the bow. After showing me the helm and various other controls, we made our way down to see the bedroom, galley, and heads. The passageway was narrow and quite short.

"It's not overly spacious, but it's perfect for what we use it for," she said before opening the bedroom door. A large queen-sized bed occupied the majority of the room. There was standing room next to the bunk, and a little more than sitting room above the mattress itself. The overnight bag I'd brought rested at the foot of the bed. By the door, a flat screen TV was mounted, with red, white, and yellow cables dangling from it, as if someone had recently unhooked a DVD player.

After showing me how to use the marine toilet, Isabel headed to the galley, and I followed. A hint of garlic butter filled the air. Tracy was standing in front of a small stove, stirring something in a medium pot. She smiled at us when we walked in. Isabel wrapped her arms around her, then kissed her neck.

"I'm almost done," Tracy said.

Isabel let go of her girlfriend, slapped her ass, and then smiled. "Tracy's quite a cook, and she's got a whole brunch menu planned for us. It's gonna be tasty! How about something to drink?" she asked me.

"Sure. What do you have?"

Tracy turned to face us and chimed in, "Champagne Mimosa?"

"Wonderful," I said, really looking forward to a refreshing drink. Although quite a few hours separated us from the midday heat, I could already feel the humid, salty air on my skin. Being in a small enclosed galley—with the stove on—certainly didn't help either.

I watched Isabel pour the champagne and orange juice into three delicate champagne flutes. She handed me one, then brought one over to Tracy.

"Here's to a fun day at sea!" she offered, raising her glass. The three of us clinked. I repeated her toast and then had a sip. The refreshing bubbly drink was delicious, and I was thirsty, so I emptied my glass in less than a minute.

"We'll get going shortly," Isabel said, taking away my flute. "Why don't you go and change in the bedroom? Tracy's nearly done in here. Come and join us back on the upper deck when you've changed clothes, okay?"

"Perfect," I said before heading to the bedroom she'd shown me a few minutes earlier. Alone, I dug into my bag. I took off my dress and underwear, then slipped on my black and white Ralph Lauren one-piece suit. I tied the white strap into a bow behind my neck. I certainly felt overdressed compared to them, but I didn't own a bikini.

A couple of seconds later, I heard the engine start.

I put my dress in my bag, then left the bedroom to join Tracy at the stern just as the boat was pulling off. A handful of young, handsome men in surfers' shorts—probably those who'd let go of the ropes that kept the yacht attached to the jetty— were waving us goodbye.

"Is this what you wear at the beach?" Tracy asked as I slid next to her onto the cushions that surrounded the table. She offered me another Mimosa.

I accepted the flute as I replied, "I don't go to the beach very often."

"You're so..." she started, then tilted her head, "...interesting," she finally settled on.

Other people had never voiced their opinions about me aloud—except for a few ex-boyfriends who never hesitated to point out my flaws. I wasn't sure how to feel about Tracy's comment, so I disregarded it.

"I think you take life too seriously, but deep down you like to have fun, no?" Tracy asked, her hand grabbing mine. "Would that be a fair assessment?"

"You're probably right," I said with a shrug.

"Stay right here," she said, squeezing my hand, then letting go of it before getting up. "I've got something that will make you relax. We're here to enjoy ourselves, right?"

I smiled and nodded. She went away, leaving me alone with my second Champagne Mimosa, which I quickly finished.

She returned a couple of minutes later with a freshly rolled joint and a silver Zippo lighter.

"This will do the trick, I promise," she said, winking at me. She lit it, then took a few puffs before passing it to me.

I can't recall the last time I smoked pot, but why not? I have to let loose, relax, and forget about my worries. Live in the moment, right?

I took her offering, brought it to my lips, and

inhaled, coughing my way through the first puff. But then it got easier. Smoking was a little like riding a bike. Although my latest smoke-free cycle had lasted years—including regular cigarettes—my body hadn't really forgotten how to smoke. Or the thrill of it. The rush it inevitably brought on.

We smoked the whole thing between the two of us, and I didn't feel anything for a few minutes. Then it hit me.

As I turned my head to watch the harbor sail by on our way out of the marina, I felt as though I'd drunk a full bottle of wine in one sitting but without the headache, the blue lips, or the slurred speech. I just felt dizzy. No, dizzy wasn't it. I felt relaxed and a little dazed. Comfortable. Happy. Really happy. Happier than I'd been in a long time.

I looked at Tracy. Her face was adorned by a large, relaxed smile; her pupils wide open even though bright sunlight reflected on the calm harbor water all around us.

"Good, right?" she asked me.

"Strong!"

She reached for the pair of black oversized sunglasses that rested on the table and put them on before returning her attention to me. "Best way to wind down!" She exhaled loudly and wrapped her arm around my shoulders and brought me closer to her. "You're really pretty, you know that, right?"

I felt my skin blush. "Thank you. And you're gorgeous."

"Ah, I wasn't saying it to receive a compliment, but thanks." She suddenly removed her arm from around me and both of her hands cupped my breasts.

I froze. *What?*

Without flinching and totally ignoring the surprised look that had to have been on my face, she asked, "You're what, a C?"

Still taken by surprise, I nodded, and she removed her hands before smiling. "Wait here. I've got something much better for you to wear." She jumped to her feet and went down below, leaving me alone and a little confused. I enjoyed my high while awaiting her return. I decided to step away from the table for a little while. I got up and leaned against the bulkhead, letting the cool ocean breeze caress my skin. The passing scenery kept my attention: lots of sailboats, speedboats, Sea-Doos, and fishing boats near us, but their numbers dwindled as we sped out to sea.

Some moments later, I was taken by surprise again when Tracy appeared next to me and reached behind my neck to untie the back of my suit. Then without any sort of warning, she took a hold of the front and pulled it down, like she was ripping a Band-Aid, exposing my breasts.

"Hey!" I yelped, instinctively crossing my arms over my chest to cover myself.

"Don't be a prude. Come on, try this on," she said, handing me a non-padded but wired, white bikini top. "It's Isabel's. I think it will work for you."

Our boat was passing near other boats, and I saw people pointing our way. *Better cover up.*

I unfolded my arms and picked up the bikini top she was offering me, concealing my breasts with the material. After adjusting the underwire to be comfortable, Tracy spun me around to tie it in the back.

"Let me have a look," she said, once again spinning me around, then taking a step back.

She clapped and jumped like a teenage girl, her small breasts bouncing up and down with a split-second delay. "Much better! Let me grab the bottom. I'll be right back."

A minute later, as promised, she returned with a

tiny piece of fabric. So tiny, in fact, I didn't even know which was the front and which was the back. Tracy probably saw the hesitation on my face and flipped the piece of clothing 180-degrees in my hands before pulling down the rest of my swimsuit, leaving me standing butt—and pussy—naked in front of her.

"Trimmed and tidy, ah!" she said. "Good, but put it on before those fishermen decide to board us," she continued, a large smile on her face as she nodded toward the left.

I turned to see what she was pointing at then gasped. We were not even one hundred feet away from the fishing boat in question. I kicked off the one-piece from around my ankles and slid on the new bottom before adjusting it into place.

"We'll have to work on your tan, girl," she said before slapping my mostly exposed ass. "You're pale as hell! But don't worry. Lots of time for that later today, and no fishermen where we're going. You won't have to be so prudish anymore." She winked at me.

Something tingled deep in me, then spread outward, warming my entire body from within. *Arousal?*

"I'll check with Isabel, but I think it's time I set this table up for brunch. Are you hungry?" Tracy asked.

"Starving," I said, not sure if I meant for food, sex, or both.

AFTER A SUMPTUOUS BRUNCH—TRACY could certainly cook some mean eggs Benedict—we headed another twenty or thirty miles farther out to sea, away from shipping lanes and pleasure boats.

The engine noise faded out. I lay down on the deck and closed my eyes, letting the calm sea rock me gently while the sun rays and light breeze caressed my skin. My straggling fears and doubts about what would likely happen today on this boat had somehow disappeared from my mind, jettisoning themselves into the chasm marijuana and alcohol had temporarily carved into my head. Life was great. I was opening myself up to new experiences.

The pop of a champagne cork took me out of my daze. When I looked up, Isabel was giggling, a large Dom Pérignon bottle in hand, trying to pour the foaming liquid into the flutes sitting on the table in front of her while Tracy was tickling her flat stomach with kisses.

"Okay, okay," Isabel said as her giggles wound down. "Drinks are ready! Come and join us," she said to me.

I stood up and took the remaining glass from the table. The girls already had theirs in hand.

Isabel turned to her girlfriend and began singing, "Happy Birthday, Tracy..." I joined in.

Tracy's cheeks were pink. A childlike quality decorated her smile. When we finished singing the last words, she clapped and jumped up. We clinked glasses and returned to the cushioned seating area.

"How old are you?" I asked the birthday girl after we sat down.

"Twenty-two," she replied. *Nearly a dozen years my junior.*

Isabel stood up and folded one section of the table before walking away. She returned with three pails half-filled with ice cubes. After tossing some of the cushions covering the seats a few feet from us, she opened a couple of hidden storage areas. She reached in to transfer water bottles into the first ice bucket, and then beer cans into the second one. After closing the storage bins and covering them with their waterproof cushions, she placed the magnum she'd opened just minutes ago into the third bucket.

"Be right back," Isabel said after moving the ice-filled containers closer to us.

Definitely won't go thirsty here.

A couple of minutes later, Isabel came back and sat on my right. She'd brought back another joint, which she lit, smoked a little, and then passed over to me.

"I want to have some fun," Tracy said on my left while I was taking a puff.

"A little later, I think," Isabel replied. I turned to look at her; her crooked smile greeted my glance.

Wow. I'm really going to go through with this?

I was pretty buzzed. Happily inebriated, not drunk—yet—but definitely high and relaxed.

"How about that cute coastguard?" I asked Tracy. "He gave you his number, right?"

She nodded. "Yes, I have it on my phone. Wanna send him some pics?"

"Sure, we could have some fun with him,"

Isabel said. "But let's warm him up nice first. Okay?"

Tracy agreed, stood up, handed me the lit joint, and then left.

I took another puff and felt Isabel's eyes on me. She said, "We like to tease good-looking men. Sometimes we do more than tease... It depends. We'll see how it goes."

Tracy returned, phone in hand, already typing something onto her screen.

"I wrote, 'Hi, handsome. I'm one of the cute blondes from the plane'," she said.

Just as she finished her sentence, her phone beeped with a reply.

"'Hi,' he wrote, with three exclamation points," Tracy reported before lifting her index finger. "He's typing something else." A pause followed. "'You girls having a good time?'"

"Tell him, 'Of course.' Let's send him a picture," Isabel suggested.

I was getting a little dizzy, turning left and right to follow along with their conversation. I passed the joint to Isabel.

"Of what?" Tracy asked excitedly.

"Let's all sit together and do a selfie of just our

tops," Isabel suggested, her eyebrows raised, a sparkle in her eyes.

"Good start," Tracy replied before pushing me closer to Isabel and aiming the phone camera at our chests. She looked at the result: champagne flutes and barely covered breasts. She smiled in approval then sent it off.

"I bet you we get a dic-pic under five," Isabel said.

"Dic-pic under five?" I asked.

"Nah, I say seven," Tracy said before turning to me. "We'll keep exposing more and more of ourselves until we get a photo of his dick. The trick is to do it without incriminating evidence or without exposing our pussies first. That's too desperate."

I laughed. *Desperate is probably right, but incriminating?* "That's not illegal..." I said, confused.

"Of course not. But we don't want too many naked pictures of ourselves on the wrong people's phones, you know? Best to leave our heads out of —" Before she could finish her train of thought, her phone beeped with a reply.

We all looked at her screen. It was a picture of his Coast Guard ship, clearly at sea, a few uniformed men standing in the shot, facing away from the camera.

"Oh, he's working," Isabel said. "We may not get the money shot from him while he's at work."

"Nah, he's a guy," I said. Maybe it was the alcohol, maybe it was the pot. Or perhaps it was intuition, but I agreed with Isabel's initial guess. "Five pics, but we have to choose them wisely. How about a picture of the two of you in bed, in bikinis, heads out of the shot?"

"Sure. Why not?" Tracy said.

A VERY SHORT bedroom photo shoot later, Tracy had about a dozen pictures to select from. I handed Tracy her phone back on the way up to the stern, and she picked the photo she liked best, then sent it off, along with the caption: 'What's missing here?'

Sebastian replied with a picture of the gun mounted at the front of his ship.

"Either he's violent or the gun's representative of his dick!" Isabel snorted.

"Come on, girls," Tracy said, getting up as though someone had lit a firecracker under her small, round ass. "What gets a guy really excited?" Her doe-eyed stare alternated between me and Isabel. We both remained silent. "Come on... A wet

T-shirt contest! I'll grab the video camera." She left running.

"Video camera? I thought you said pictures could be incriminating. Wouldn't videos be worse?" I asked, confused.

Isabel shook her head while finishing the last bit of our latest joint. "We use an old-fashioned mini-camcorder with tapes. There's only one copy of the tape and we control it. We're fine with that."

"Okay. But I don't have a white T-shirt."

"No need. That top you've got on, it gets really transparent when wet. It's not lined at all. In fact, I can already see your nipples through it. You have nice tits," she said, gently cupping them, caressing them through the fabric of the borrowed bikini top. A muted thrill came over me. She let go of me for a second to dip her right hand in the bucket closest to us. She then brought a half-melted ice cube to my left breast.

I instantly felt the chill of it, my flesh reacting instantly to the frozen surface, hardening. She made circular motions with the cube around my nipple, the ice quickly melting to expose my areola through the now transparent fabric.

"See? What did I tell you," Isabel said.

I grabbed my own breast, staring at it as though I'd never seen it before.

And come to think of it, I've probably never seen it like that, in broad day light, in the middle of the ocean.

Tracy came back, having traded her hot-pink bikini top for a cropped, white tank top. Her small nipples perked through the fabric. She frowned at Isabel after seeing what she had done to the top I was wearing.

"Don't worry, I wouldn't start without you here, baby," Isabel said, her words bringing Tracy's angled eyebrows back to their regular, softer positions. "It will dry before we get started, I promise. I'm going to have a beer and maybe smoke another one." She bent to grab a can from the bucket and handed me one.

Although I was really tipsy and pretty high as well, I couldn't resist. It was just too hot. I grabbed the can she offered.

TEN MINUTES, a happy smoke, and a beer later, my bikini top was dry, as promised.

Isabel even rubbed my nipple to prove it to Tracy. "See? Fabric's solid white again. Just like before. No harm, no foul."

Save for my arousal, which was still climbing.

It was weird hanging out with two women who were so comfortable with their sexuality. Touching a stranger's most private body parts seemed... natural to them.

And to be fair, taking part in their game has certainly been enjoyable so far. I've always liked men that's for sure, but a little part of me's very curious. These two women here

*are wonderful specimens. Young, firm bodies, sensual, and...
very open-minded.*

After grabbing my empty can out of my hand,
Isabel broke the silence. "Who's first?" she asked. "I
vote for our new friend," she said, nodding in my
direction.

She paused briefly, but Tracy and I stayed quiet.

"Tracy, why don't you hook up the camera on
the post, and then we'll be able to record all three
of us doing it together. Okay, baby?"

Tracy lifted her thumb, got up, and then
proceeded to attach their camera to the existing
tripod.

How many videos do they record out here?

Tracy walked away for a few minutes, then came
back with a new ice bucket. She knelt down by the
other pails and moved the empty magnum, water
bottles, and beer cans out of the old ice buckets,
transferring the ones that were still full to a fourth
bucket, filled with fresh ice, that she'd just brought out.

The birthday girl then relocated behind the
camera and adjusted the direction in which it
pointed. As ordered by Tracy, Isabel and I carried
the older, waterier buckets to the exact spots they
needed to go.

I'd never done a wet T-shirt contest before, but had nothing against them. Prize or not, the idea of it was exciting, and I could definitely cool off.

"Perfect. We've got the sun behind the camera," Tracy said. "Not another boat in sight. Just us girls. What do you say we have ourselves some fun?" Tracy's pitch had increased so much over the past few sentences I could have believed she was leading a pot legalization rally.

Isabel and I hooted in unison. "Anything for the birthday girl!" I added.

"I hope so," Tracy said, grazing my waist with a finger just as she passed behind me to grab the ice bucket. A shiver ran through me. "Stand right here," she ordered, pointing me to a spot in front of her, just a foot away from where I currently was.

I obeyed and she continued. "Now, both of you look at that camera and flirt with it, tease it with everything you've got. Shake those girls."

I joined Isabel's hoots and screams. We cheered like we were two teenage girls at a boy-band concert. Isabel was standing next to me, raising her breasts toward the sky, feeling them, letting her fingers slip underneath the tiny triangles of fabric that covered her nipples. I did the same.

We were just girls, having fun, acting a little crazy and not hurting anyone.

Then... I felt it.

Tracy, who had been standing behind us the entire time—letting the tripod take care of the recording for her—poured the entire ice-cold slushy mixture over my head, the top of my chest getting the bulk of it, my top totally transparent. I was so frozen—from both the shock and temperature—that my shoulders automatically recoiled forward. Tracy's hands came from behind and pulled my shoulders back, then massaged my breasts.

"Let us see your magnificent tits, girl," she ordered. "And smile, you're on camera!"

2:30 P.M.

TRACY'S HANDS gave my breasts a final squeeze, then Isabel slapped my and her girlfriend's ass at the same time.

"Your turn, Tracy," Isabel ordered.

I moved aside and Tracy took front stage. Isabel stood behind her, ice bucket at the ready.

Tracy was playing her part, flirting with the camera, zigzagging the bottom edge of her tiny top upward and downward sensually, at times exposing the curvature at the base of her breasts, but never her nipples—or at least not for longer than a split second. She then pulled the fabric downward to stretch it and arched her back. Isabel dumped the bucket's contents on her. Tracy let out a high-pitch squeal and Isabel's hands joined hers in exposing what her tiny T-shirt had previously kept hidden from the naked eye.

After a minute or so of stroking, Tracy turned her head to steal a kiss from Isabel, and then they traded spots. "Your turn, baby."

Tracy turned to me. "Why don't you do the honors this time," she asked, winking. "You've seen how we do it. Easy, right?"

"Sure," I said, eager to reciprocate the painfully delicious sensations I'd just experienced, and... partly curious to see which of Isabel or Tracy had the best rack.

Isabel started her performance as if she were teasing an invisible cameraman—or woman. Just as she raised her chest in anticipation for the cold shower, I dumped the melted ice cubes all over her. She screeched and then backed onto me, her hands grabbing mine and forcing me to touch her, to knead her breasts, some of my fingers over and others under the little triangles of fabric. Then, she grabbed one of my hands and moved it down to her pussy. I was in uncharted territory; the only pussy I'd ever known was mine, but I let my fingers graze the fabric of her bikini bottom.

Tracy joined us. She kissed Isabel, sandwiching

her between us. Tracy's arms then reached down my back, and she grabbed a handful of my ass, pulling me closer to Isabel, but making her lose footing. We crashed together on the deck, laughing.

Although such a fall on an epoxy surface should have been at least a little painful, I suspect our level of intoxication softened it. Our high certainly made it hard for us to stop laughing or groping each other.

"That's perfect for number three! Hold on," Tracy said, springing back to her feet to snatch her phone from the nearby table and then crashing back down next to us. She extended her arm in the air for another selfie, then showed us the results: a beautiful mid-chest shot—no heads in sight—with six hardened nipples, five of which were covered by transparent fabric, plus one of Isabel's magnificent, natural C-cups fully exposed. Our fall—or my hands?—must have pushed the puny triangle out of position.

"What will you say to that, Sebastian?" Tracy asked rhetorically just after she hit the SEND button.

Her phone beeped a couple of seconds later. "Ah! He's asking, 'Who's the third?'"

"Hot flight at-ten-dant," Tracy replied, saying

the syllables aloud as she typed the letters into her phone. She then sent it off.

The next beep had the three of us staring at Tracy's screen: 'Can I come over for dessert?'

"Now we're talking!" Isabel said, a large smile on her face. Her hand had somehow moved and was now rubbing my groin. "Dic-pic in no time," she said, her eyes locked onto mine. Isabel's touch was far more gentle than that of most men who'd rubbed my pussy before, yet it was precise and firm. I didn't know if the pot had anything to do with how aroused I was, but Isabel was turning me on, making me wet my bottom.

"'De-pends on what you're bring-ing'," Tracy was once again saying the words aloud as she typed them.

"Oh! That's good, baby," Isabel said before kissing her.

A few minutes elapsed. The girls couldn't stop giggling. They had come up with various 'salami' variations he could have replied with, but since his answer had yet to arrive, they were convinced that Sebastian was now busy making himself hard in the heads somewhere on his ship. *Of course, he'd have to send us a picture he was proud of!*

Once our giggling wound down, Isabel returned

to caressing my pussy, but her fingers had now slid under the fabric. She was kissing her girlfriend, her finger tickling my clit, when the phone beeped again: 'Where are you?' was his reply.

"Guess he's coming!" Tracy squealed. "Where are we, baby?" she asked her girlfriend, tapping her on the chest like an excited kid tugging on his mother's sleeve. Isabel spurted out a latitude and a longitude and Tracy typed the numbers in, and then sent them off.

Tracy sat up. "I'm so excited. I haven't seen a dick in so long!" She turned to me and added, "I bet his is nice and big, you know?" She bit her lips. Her hands flew in the air, and she held them about nine inches apart, just to clarify her expectations.

Isabel sat up as well, taking her hand out of my bikini bottom. "Come on, Tracy. Don't exaggerate. Remember that firefighter I found for you a few months ago? He had a nice, big cock, right? You liked him."

"Ooooh, I'd forgotten about him." Tracy smiled, jumping to her feet. She pulled Isabel, then me up from the deck. "Let's go. I want to watch him again. He's hot."

"Whatever you want, birthday girl!" Isabel said.

She then walked to the video camera, turned off the recording, and detached the device. "Let's go."

Isabel grabbed my hand and escorted me below deck to their bedroom.

"Make yourself comfortable. I just have to attach this to the TV and find the right tape," she said indicating to the camera she was still holding. "You want to smoke some more? Tracy's out back, having a few more puffs."

"No, I'm good," I said, probably with a stupid, happy smile on my face. I hadn't felt that relaxed in... forever. I brushed my hand against my own skin. It felt different, almost as if someone else was touching me. I caressed my own stomach, letting my hand slip down to my bikini bottom. With my other hand, I brought my hair up behind my head, leaving it in a messed-up chignon that would fall the second I moved, but it freed up my neck. My own fingers on the nape of my neck felt oh-so-delicious right now, even though I knew they were mine.

If getting high could be measured in terms of floors, I had reached my penthouse; nothing too crazy, nothing too plain... And I was *so* horny.

I kept touching myself, waiting for Isabel to find the right tape. She finally did. She paused it and then joined me on the bed while we waited for

Tracy to return. We kept ourselves occupied with light kisses and caresses, but when I turned my back to her, asking her to undo the intricately knotted strings in the back, she stopped me.

"No, Tracy would kill me. You're her birthday present. You know that, right?" Isabel paused. I raised my shoulders, then she continued, "She has to unwrap you, even if there isn't much left to the imagination," she said, winking. "I'm looking forward to the official unwrapping," she told me before leaning onto me, her lips firm and demanding.

"Hey! Don't start without me!" Tracy said from the foot of the bed a second later.

"Don't worry, baby. Just hit **PLAY** on the camera. It's ready to go."

Tracy did just as ordered and squeezed herself between me and Isabel, her hands on each of our laps.

The girls were pretty good actresses, it turned out.

In this brief recording, Tracy—while cooking in nothing but an old, cropped T-shirt—had inadvertently left the burner on, and a small galley fire had erupted. (To be clear, there was no actual fire involved in the movie.) The brave firefighter came in, uniform and all, to save the day, and take off her burning clothes, of course! And once the day had been saved, the good Samaritan had to be paid off for his services, but it was overtime for him, so he'd required double payment—i.e., double pussy. And so, Isabel had then joined them in front of the camera.

They were right.

That firefighter's cock was splendid. And he also knew what to do with it.

I felt myself getting wet just watching him fuck Tracy on TV. His large dick thrusting into her pussy, the same pussy that had distracted me and made me blush at work yesterday.

Then, my attention got sidetracked.

Tracy's fingers had slid their way past the lining of my soaking-wet bikini bottom.

With one of her hands in her own bikini and the other stroking my pussy, Tracy sat on top of my lap. She then retrieved both of her hands from our clothing and motioned for Isabel to do something with the camera. Tracy brought her hands to my face. She leaned toward me, then kissed me on the lips, biting me gently, her tongue licking mine. Then, her appetite increased. She moved down to my neck, whispering something I couldn't quite make out, but the feel of her breath against my neck was inebriating. She sat back up then let her fingertips dance around my breasts for a while, teasing but never quite grasping them the way I wanted... yet.

Her lips then returned to my chest. This time, they were more demanding. Her hands pulled the fabric up, exposing my breasts, which were heaving with insatiable hunger. She nibbled on one of my nipples while squeezing the other with the exact pressure I wanted to feel. I let out a moan. I reached for her top and pulled it down. She abandoned me for just a few seconds while she untied her top. Tracy then tossed the unwanted clothing away toward Isabel, who was busy filming us. I gently cupped Tracy's small, beautiful breasts, then sat up so I could kiss them and grant them the attention they deserved. I felt her arms reach behind me, and suddenly my bikini top fell lose between us.

Tracy pushed me back down. My back landed on the mattress, my breasts bouncing for a couple of seconds from the unexpected movement. I then watched her walk backwards on all fours, her eyes locked on me, her hanging breasts gently swaying as she backed toward my legs, taking with her the only piece of clothing I was still wearing. She brushed a gentle kiss on my pussy on the way down, her breath tickling me. However, once the bottom cleared my ankles, Tracy came back with a serious appetite. Her pointy tongue and agile fingers knew exactly what to do with my womanhood.

I couldn't help but let her.

I felt a little lazy lying there, unable to do anything but thoroughly enjoy her licking me, fucking me with her tongue, then with her fingers. Every now and then, I'd manage to open my eyes, my own chest surprising me in how much it was moving. I was breathing hard, moaning, enjoying every lick, every prick, every kiss from the woman laying between my legs. I reached down to brush her hair, massaging her scalp, not knowing how to return the pleasure she was filling me with when she looked up, and her eyes met mine.

Her tongue circled her lips, then she made her way toward my chest, still straddling me. I reached to pull down her bottoms. The familiar blonde landing strip was just a foot away from my face. She briefly rolled over to one side, letting one leg out of her bikini bottom, then returned to the straddling position, inching her pussy toward my mouth. I grabbed a second pillow and placed it under my neck and let her lower herself onto my face. For the first time ever, my tongue explored the most secretive part of another woman. Her moans became more frequent and louder as I learned what she liked. I suckled. I licked. I poked her with my tongue. I gently nibbled on her lips then brought along my hands on this inaugural, explorative experience.

A few minutes later, I felt a weight near the foot of the mattress. I came up for air and looked past Tracy's narrow hips. Isabel had put down the camera on the corner by the TV, its small light still flashing red. It seemed like Isabel had decided to partake in the birthday festivities and was now making her way up to me, licking and caressing my inner thighs. Just as she was getting seriously busy with my genitals, Tracy called out her name.

Isabel abandoned my pussy and straddled my stomach, kneeling behind Tracy. One of Isabel's hands grabbed her girlfriend's breasts from behind and brought her body closer to hers, pressing Tracy's back against her chest. Isabel's other hand went to Tracy's ass an inch from my face. I saw her thrust a couple of fingers up Tracy's ass just as she was about to come.

I teased her pussy with my tongue for a few

seconds longer, but her muscles contracted and she pulled up, then sat just below my breasts. She exhaled loudly, a large grin on her rosy face. After pressing her hands firmly onto my tits, Tracy said, "Best. Birthday. Ever," each of her words accentuated by a push of her hands.

"Can we make this an annual tradition?" she asked. She wasn't addressing me, but Isabel, who was still kneeling behind her.

"We'll see, babe," Isabel said, slapping Tracy's ass.

Tracy lifted her right leg then pivoted away from me before jumping out of bed. "I'm going to dive in the ocean to cool off for just a second. Be right back," she said before running up to the main deck, butt naked.

"You don't mind if I have your leftovers then?" Isabel shouted out toward the bedroom door.

A few seconds later, not having heard a bleep from Tracy, Isabel turned to me and said, "I guess she doesn't mind." Then she leaned over me and pressed her lips against mine.

After a delicious kiss, she licked her way down my body, back to her previous position, her tanned ass now perked up in the air. She spread my legs wide, then lowered herself to sit on one of my knees, her wet pussy rubbing onto me as she fingered me with one, then two digits. I lowered my hand and started playing with my clit. Her hips were riding my knee at the same cadence as her fingers were fucking me. I started flicking my clit more rapidly, about to come when Tracy came back into the bedroom.

"Girls?" she said. It took a minute for my mind to register the strange tone in Tracy's voice. I ignored the distraction until I finished quivering.

Clapping sounds then echoed through the small bedroom. Multiple sets of hands. Multiple people were clapping.

"What the...?" Isabel asked, turning around as I sat up to look at Tracy, curious as to how she could have made those noises by herself.

I gasped when I saw five skinny Afro-Hispanic men, with rifles, standing behind Tracy, whose arms were raised above her head. Her entire naked body was shivering.

The coastguard's warning echoed in my mind, but the hard reality prevented noises from escaping my mouth. *Pirates? What now?*

"Money. Key. For boat. Now!" the man standing in front of them said before the butt of his rifle pushed Tracy's back, and she fell onto the bed with us.

"One minute," Isabel said, her hands covering herself the best she could. I did the same with whatever portion of the bedsheets I could grab. Tracy just sat there, as though frozen.

Images of my own body floating in the deep blue ocean, a bullet hole through the chest, flooded my mind. I started thinking about my past. I had begun my last stroll down memory lane when a loud horn sounded in the distance.

The man who had asked for the money and keys turned to face his crew and ordered the man at the back to do something in a language I didn't recognize. If it was Spanish, it was a dialect I didn't know. The man furthest back ran toward the upper deck, then returned a couple of seconds later, screaming. All five men left right then and there, without our money, without the boat's keys, and—thankfully—without killing any of us.

"What scared them?" Isabel asked, making her way toward the tiny porthole on one side of the bed, then the other.

I wrapped my arms around Tracy, who had come out of her trance and who was now crying her heart out.

"Worst... birthday... ever," she said in between sobs.

"Did they touch you?" I asked her. She shook her head. I wrapped my arms around her shivering body and rocked her gently. "It will be fine. We'll all be fine, Tracy."

"The fucking coastguard's here!" Isabel exclaimed. "Sebastian sent us something much better than a dic-pic. We should probably get dressed before another group of men sees us naked," she said.

I laughed. Maybe it was my nerves, maybe I was still high. One thing was for sure: I was glad to be alive.

Less than two minutes later, we were dressed again and back on the upper deck, watching none other than Sebastian himself coming up to our yacht in a small boat that had likely been dispatched by the larger ship we could see a few miles away.

He came onboard and inquired if we were alright.

"Thanks to you," Tracy said. "They came onboard, with weapons. I thought they were going to kill us."

"I know. That's what I was warning you about on the plane. But you're okay?"

We all nodded and he was about to step back into his boat when Tracy stopped him. "Hold on a sec, will you?"

Sebastian shook his head, then pointed at the pirates' speedboat that was dashing away, soon to disappear off of the horizon. "I don't have much time; we need to go after them."

"It will just take a sec, I swear. It'll be worth it."

She came back about ten seconds later, a small video tape in hand. "You'll have to rewind it and find an old camcorder to play it in, but consider that your *dessert* and thank-you present," Tracy said before giving him a big hug and kissing him on the cheek.

After letting go of her embrace, he sent a curious smile her way, then toward Isabel. He tucked away the tape into one of his uniform pockets and stepped back into his boat.

We thanked him again and waved at our savior as his boat sped away.

BACK IN THE safety of my airport hotel room, my marijuana-induced mental fog now fully dissipated, I couldn't help but reflect on what had happened yesterday and today.

Sure, I hadn't been able to meet with Matt, my friend-with-benefits, but the weekend had nonetheless included sex and had offered... a transformative experience.

I'd never thought I'd ever have a threesome, let alone a lesbian encounter in my lifetime. But those two women... They were so sensual, so comfortable with their bodies, so beautiful.

But what does it mean?

Am I gay, now?

No. Definitely not.

I didn't think a pussy could ever fulfill me as much as a glorious cock could, but today's experience... It was something I'd like to try again (aside from the pirate part).

Exhausted, I put down my journal and closed my eyes.

Images of pirates, sexy coastguards, and beautiful blonde women started to populate my emerging dreams...

PART TWO

MY XXX EXPERIENCE

THE PLAN

FOR THE RECORD, let's just state that I don't want to risk getting caught by modern seafaring thieves who call themselves pirates, but I would sure as hell like to get my hands on that video tape. In order to do that, I have to pick my approach among the three trails left behind by my mystery stewardess:

OPTION 1: Canvass all airlines that fly into Cancun, Mexico, and find either an ex-flight attendant called Matt or a female one called Kate, either of which could identify my stewardess.

I've got nothing to go on here. CUN/Cancun is

the second busiest airport in all of Mexico. Too many airlines and chartered flights to count. Worse odds than finding red-headed Alex in Toronto.

Likelihood of success: Nil.

OPTION 2: Go to Cancun and find the hot blondes who could direct me to my mystery woman.

At least I have a name for both the boat and the marina. But boats can easily be relocated to another port or stay out in international waters. That being said, those blondes don't strike me as survivalists who would go out to sea for months at a time and brave tropical storms. I'm hoping they haven't slipped to another marina yet. And if they have, I could try and follow the trail left behind by various utility or jetty receipts associated with their yacht.

Likelihood of success: Average to high.

OPTION 3: Find coastguard Sebastian.

I looked up various organizations in charge of patrolling Mexican waters. Sebastian must be with the *Búsqueda y Rescate Marítimo*, the Mexican Search and Rescue organization. Unfortunately, I don't have many contacts south of the border who could help me with that. But maybe the two hot blondes still have his cellphone number? Possibly. Wouldn't they want to stay in touch with the guy who saved their lives (and who could maybe do it again?)

Likelihood of success: Average, but I'd have to succeed with Option 2 first.

This time, I should have enough to find her. I know the name of the boat, the marina, and the town. All I have to do is take a short flight to Cancun and track them down. Easy peasy. Mystery solved.

...Or so I thought.

WHAT HAPPENED

CAN/CANCUN is one of my regular stops, so I figured I could track down the girls on any of my layovers. I could deadhead home a few hours after getting the information I'm looking for. No need to take extra time off.

I landed in Cancun on a sunny Monday afternoon. After clearing customs, I stopped by the currency exchange booth, then rented a convertible from one of the car companies operating out of the airport.

A large smile on my face, still wearing my pilot's uniform, and quite a few *pesos* in my wallet, I made my way to *La Esperanza Marina*. Nothing like breathing in the salty, humid Caribbean air with the top down to get my hopes up.

Here's how my Mexican adventure unfolded.

6:16 P.M.

FINDING the marina and the *Delicious Sunset* was easy.

Although it wasn't the largest motorboat in this harbor, the beautiful yacht appeared luxurious alongside its neighboring, smaller pleasure boats.

Isabel's family has to be fairly wealthy.

I turned a few heads walking on the jetty in my pilot's uniform, but I didn't care. I certainly would have been a little more comfortable in shorts, like most of the people I saw hanging around here, but I only expected to drop in, get the info I needed, then head back out. The sun was about to set anyway, so the heat should go away soon.

Now standing in front of their boat, I called out

from the jetty, but no one answered. I walked alongside the boat, heading toward the stern and then tried again. "Hi there, Isabel? Tracy? Are you onboard?"

The boat was tidied up. I could see the patio-area where the girls had partied, but no sign of life. I decided to turn around and make my way back toward the bow and the boat's walkway.

Is it appropriate for me to step onboard?

I had my hand on the guardrail, about to step forward on the walkway when a balding man in his fifties wearing plaid shorts and an oversized tank top draping over a beer belly walked up to me.

"Hey there. Where you going?" he asked.

I stepped back onto the public jetty, let go of the guardrail, and then brought my right hand in the air. "Hey, man. I'm just looking for Isabel and Tracy. Is this their boat?" I asked, pointing at the yacht.

"Ya. That's the one. But the ladies ain't here." The man crossed his tattooed arms on his chest, then stepped closer to me, blocking my path to the walkway.

I backed off some more, waving my hands in the air like two white flags. Although I was in better shape than him, there was no telling if he was crazy.

I didn't want to risk getting into a fight. "No worries, man! I'm not gonna go onboard if they're not here."

The man stood still, his expressionless eyes riveted on my face. I glanced around for a few seconds and realized we had attracted quite a few stares from nearby boaters.

"I'm gonna get going, but any idea where I could find them?"

The fat man remained silent. I gave up and turned around, ready to walk away when a woman's voice addressed me from a nearby boat. "The girls headed out to a bar about an hour ago to celebrate one thing or another," she said.

I released a breath I hadn't realized I was holding, then headed, smiling, toward the elderly, red-headed woman in the flowery sundress.

"Thank you, ma'am. Do you, by any chance, happen to know the name of that bar?" I asked her.

"*Pacifico*, I think," said a seventy-odd-year-old man who'd suddenly appeared from behind the red-headed woman.

I decided to push my luck just a tad more. "I'm not from 'round here. Would you happen to know where this *Pacifico* place is?"

He scratched his head, worsening the messy state of his gray hair. "Roughly, sure. Exactly, no."

"I'll take rough directions," I said, pleasantly surprised.

He turned to face the town, and then pointed at the church. "About four blocks that way," he started, then he moved his hand toward the right before continuing, "Then two or three that way, I think."

Mental note made of the bar's rough location, I thanked the helpful neighbors, and then left the marina.

6:58 P.M.

SALSA MUSIC RESONATED past the entrance.

I pulled open the door to *Pacifico* and the volume tripled. *Who goes out dancing this early?* On my way in, I walked past a large Mexican man who stood, arms crossed, blocking a large wooden door. Next to him was what seemed to be a coat check counter where a young Latina worked, tagging empty coat hangers. She smiled at me as I walked by. I'd left my hat in the trunk of the car. No need for her services. The bouncer/doorman eyed me up and down but otherwise stayed motionless. I kept going.

No cover, I guess.

A few steps later, the room opened up in front of me. Flashing red, green, and blue lights bounced on the mirrored walls that surrounded a dance floor at the back of the room. A DJ sat in the far left corner, behind two large speakers that acted as supports for the flat plank that held his equipment. On the far right corner was a small bar. A tall and skinny man dressed in black stood behind it, wiping its surface. Half the stools were occupied by Latinos who were scoping out the local dance talent. A few round tables dotted the area surrounding the dance floor, where women of various skin shades sat, heads bobbing to the rhythm, sipping colorful drinks that came with umbrellas. Oddly enough, the majority of them were blondes. Bleached blondes.

I decided to join the male-occupied bar as it offered the best vantage point. I sat myself on the left-most stool, leaving some breathing room between me and a perfume-deluged, curly-haired Latino in ripped jean shorts and a fluorescent yellow top.

Once seated, the bartender acknowledged my presence with a nod. I yelled out my order, trying to overbear the loud music, "Gin tonic, *por favor.*"

The barman nodded again, then turned to grab a bottle of gin with a label I'd never seen before. He returned to me a minute later, placed my mixed drink on a small, square, white paper napkin, and then voiced the amount I owed him, which I didn't understand. I sat up from my stool, reached for my wallet, then took out a two-hundred-peso bill and handed it to him. He walked to his register, then came back with some change. I dropped a few coins in the prominent tip jar—the establishment had obviously integrated their northern neighbor's capitalist ways—then put the rest of the change in my wallet before sitting again, this time facing the dance floor.

Picking out two lesbian blondes shouldn't be too hard, right? Just have to wait for them to kiss each other on the mouth, and I'll know who to approach. Patience is all I need here. Patience, Charlie.

A busty blonde shook her hips and generous booty a few feet from me. She was dancing with a skinny man half her size. Her skin rolled underneath her leopard-print top, even though her legs were slender. I took a sip of my drink, then continued scoping the dance floor. I spotted a couple of decent-looking twenty-something blondes dancing together, close to the DJ. Not as breath-taking or as gorgeous as I expected them to be based on my stewardess's diary entry, but hey... Maybe they'd put on weight since meeting my mystery woman. Maybe encountering pirates on the high-seas had had some sort of post-traumatic effect whose only cure turned out to have been ice cream and cake.

I pivoted on my stool, intent on ordering them drinks: a great way to break the ice. I had another two-hundred-peso bill in my hand and was waiting for the barman's attention when a velvety voice sounded behind me, "*Hola, capitán.*"

I got up from my stool and turned around. A gorgeous, young, petite woman with bright-blue hair was staring at me. She had on a very short red dress with a scoop neck exposing something I wanted to see more of. I racked my brain for a second. *Is this someone I've met before?* I was a little lost for words—interrupted in my plan to approach the blonde lesbians—so I settled for the obvious.

"Do I know you?" I yelled out over the song that was finally winding down.

"No. I wanted to ask if you were a pilot, but..." she said before extending her arm and then patting the left side of my jacket, where my wings were pinned down, "...I see that you are," she finished with a smile, a little shrug, and a few too many flicks of those mascara-covered eyelashes to mean nothing.

I sat back down on my seat, lowering myself so I wouldn't tower so much over her short height. I leaned forward toward her, partly so she could hear me over the latest song that had just come on, partly because I wanted an excuse to bring my face closer to her, to catch a drift of her scent, and, of course, to peek down that cleavage without her knowing a thing about it.

"You... like pilots?" I asked her, taking in her tit-town scenery from above.

The blue-haired girl moved in closer, then her finger slowly traced the crease in the middle of my pant leg, from my knee all the way to the fold of my thigh. "Yes. You could say that... But I'm not here for me. My... friend *really* likes pilots, but she's shy. I thought I could invite you to our table and introduce you to her. If you don't mind. I can buy you a drink for your trouble," she said before moving away from my ear, her lashes batting again to accentuate her bright blue eyes.

I leaned in. "Where's your friend?" I asked.

She somehow squeezed herself between my partially parted legs, then gently turned my neck toward the back of the room. With her index finger, she pointed to an athletic-looking blonde in tight, shiny red pants and a black tank top sitting alone at a table in the back.

I thought about it for a second.

Should I join two hot chicks who dig pilots—an option which would probably result in a very happy ending for me—or should I approach the average-looking lesbians who hold the information I need? It's not like they're sailing away this minute. I can go and meet them on their boat first thing tomorrow morning...

I smiled at the blue-haired woman. "Why not?"

I stuffed my money back in my wallet, then got up from my stool. She smiled then grabbed my hand and pulled me away from my seat. My near-empty drink in my other hand, I ogled her long legs and red heels as I followed her to her friend's table.

THE GIRL in the red dress walked over to her seated friend and said something to her that the loud music made impossible for me to overhear.

Her blonde friend stood up, then reached her hand out toward me, her lips moving but the words not reaching my ears. The DJ's decibel output was over-the-top, especially considering the time of day and how empty the bar was.

I could ask her to repeat herself, but chances are I still wouldn't hear it over the loud music.

My hand met hers in a shake. "I'm Charlie, airline pilot. Nice to meet you," I shouted.

The blonde girl had a wide smile on her face. She motioned for me to sit down. I grabbed a chair from a nearby table and moved it next to her before taking a seat.

The blue-haired woman lifted the Modelo bottle in front of her friend, then shook it, meeting her eyes. The blonde nodded. The blue-haired woman then tapped me on the arm before leaning in and then pointing at my glass. "What is it?" she yelled near my ear.

"Gin Tonic," I replied loudly.

She nodded, then walked away.

Part of me felt awkward letting a woman buy me a drink. Not typical for me. I made too much money to let that happen. But then again, perhaps women who dyed their hair bright blue liked to take charge and buy men drinks?

I could always return the favor on the next round. Gives me an excuse for chatting them up longer if my natural charms don't melt away their resistance as quickly as they should.

The blonde woman moved her chair closer to mine, then placed her hand on my arm before leaning in and voicing something inaudible, yet again.

I cupped my ear with my hand, and then raised my shoulders.

"Want to dance?" she asked, this time, over-articulating her words and yelling loud enough to cover the rhythmic music.

I frowned and shook my head.

I'd rather admit defeat now than make myself look like a fool. At least the uniform gives me a pretty-good chance at nailing one of them tonight. That hope would dissipate if they saw my lack of coordination on the dance floor. I can dance, kind of. But next to Latino men? Not a chance in hell.

The following minute was a tad awkward.

What can you do in a bar when you can't talk or dance?

The blonde tilted her head, staring at me, possibly sizing me up. Out of nowhere, she grabbed my left hand and pinched my naked ring finger. I looked up at her. I believe her lips motioned, "Not married?"

I shook my head.

Her smile got bigger, then she bit her lower lip. Blondie got up, then sat on my lap. Wrapping her arms around my neck, she engulfed me with her sweet, fruity scent. Her lips touched my ear. "No girlfriend or otherwise engaged for this evening?" she asked before pulling back to make eye contact with me.

I shook my head slowly and watched a strange hunger swell in her eyes.

Too easy. I love women who fantasize about pilots.

Just then, the hot, blue-haired fox in the red dress came back to the table, holding two beer bottles in one hand and my clear drink in the other.

"Here you go," her lips appeared to say while handing me the drink. I thanked her and she shrugged. She then handed her friend one of the bottles and held hers up in the air. Her lips moved again, but I didn't catch what she'd said. I nonetheless raised and clanked my glass against their bottles.

To a fun evening...

The blue-haired woman sat and looked at the blonde and me. Her friend was now kissing my ear, her fingers massaging my scalp. I met the blue-haired woman's eyes. She too had that hunger in her eyes.

Are they both into me? Could this lead to...?

Just as the thought entered my mind, the current song came to an end and the blonde sitting on my lap asked, "Want to come with us elsewhere?"

Hell, yeah!

I nodded. My last threesome was probably a decade ago. And I don't recall the willing parties being that hot. The blue-haired woman downed her beer, her eyes locked onto mine. Blondie got up from my lap and did the same.

I normally enjoyed sipping my gin, but I didn't want to risk having them change their mind. I quickly swallowed what was left of my gifted booze. As I put my empty glass down on the table, Blondie gripped my hand and pulled me up. I followed Blondie's hurried step away from the table, the blue-haired fox in tow.

When we reached the lobby, the bouncer's previous blank expression turned into a crooked smile and a nod my way.

Does he know these two?

He stepped sideways, clearing the door behind him. The Latina in the coat check buzzed it open.

What the fuck?

Blondie pushed the door and a tall staircase appeared in front of us. She hurried upstairs. I watched her small ass in those shiny red pants and felt my cock nod in approval. I kept going up, following her booty like a horse racing for its carrot.

When I reached the top of the stairs, Blondie turned around and the blue-haired fox grabbed my ass.

"Wanna have some fun?" Blondie asked. This time the music was muffled by the door one floor below. It must have closed on its own. I was able to hear her silky, sensual voice. The bass still reverberated loudly through the floor, but it only served to turn me on even more.

"Who's first?" I asked.

7:55 P.M.

BLONDIE DUG a silver key out of her red pant pocket, then unlocked one of the two doors that stood at the top of the staircase.

What kind of cheap hotel is this? Do they live here?

She pushed the door open, then her hand blindly felt the inside wall. A light turned on a second later to illuminate a bare room with a double mattress lying in the middle of it. The unmade bed was covered with white sheets, albeit stained ones. Tethered paisley wallpaper adorned the wall in front of me. Blondie held the door open while I stepped in. On the right side was nothing but a bare window protected by rusty steel bars; across from it was a crooked painting of a bad landscape faded by years of exposure to direct sunlight. I blinked and wasn't sure if I saw cockroaches running along the seam where the wall met the orange, cigarette-burn-scarred carpet. A lingering aroma of incense filled the air.

But just when the gloomy surroundings were starting to downgrade my excitement, Blondie took her top off and tossed it on the bed behind her. She started dancing to the salsa rhythm that was permeating the room from underneath. She didn't wear a bra under her top; she didn't need one. Her small, firm breasts were perky, naturally. Blue-haired girl joined her and started dancing behind her, her hands all over Blondie's newly exposed, cute little breasts and flat stomach. Blondie was shaking her tits, tossing them to the intoxicating rhythm, her skinny but muscular arms up in the air while the other woman's hands reached from behind her and undid her red pants: first unbuttoning the silver clip, then unzipping the fastener. Blue-Hair let her hands slide down her friend's pants, caressing her ass, her pussy. My mind was flying at a thousand miles a minute; my cock was hard, pushing against my uniform.

I didn't know if it was Ricky Martin, Enrique Iglesias, or some other Latino pop artist who was responsible for these beats, but I would have given him my future first-born right now, no questions asked.

Blue-Hair slowly pulled down her friend's pants, revealing the tiniest of red-stringed panties. I could no longer stand still. I started walking toward the blonde beauty dancing in front of me. But her friend left her stripping-duty-post behind Blondie when she saw me move. She ran to me and stopped me in my path. She brought her arms to my neck and loosened my tie, then danced slowly backwards, still holding on to the ends of it. When I returned my attention to her friend, the red pants had come off. She was now facing away from me, shaking her tiny booty to the music, her firm butt cheeks, barely separated by a red string, calling my name.

Blue-Hair joined Blondie, then it was Blondie's turn to help get her friend naked. She moved behind Blue-Hair and got a hold of the bottom of her red dress, shaking it, tossing it upward and downward with the salsa rhythm. I saw a flash of blonde pussy.

I started moving forward again, as if guided by where my hardened cock wanted to point, but both women shook their heads, sending me disapproving looks. I stayed put but started unbuttoning my jacket. Their frowns flipped upward. Blondie's hands left the bottom of the red dress and instead, dove into the front of her friend's scoop neck and dug out one of her tits.

Natural. Round. Perky.

I tossed my jacket on the floor, then loosened my tie some more before pulling it off fully. I was now undoing my white uniform shirt, my finger quickly unfastening each of the buttons while Blondie's hand brought out her friend's other tit.

It was too much for me.

I threw my shirt onto the carpet, then crossed the few steps that were separating us in a split second, not caring whether or not they wanted to keep that tease cycle going.

I pushed both of them onto the bed. I undid my belt, unzipped my pants, and then dug out my swollen cock. A quick glance at their faces indicated they were as eager as I was. Blue-Hair had landed with her legs spread open, her blonde pussy winking at me, so I went for it. But Blondie intercepted me, wrapping her lips on my cock before I could dip it into her friend. Blue-Hair's hands reached for my face and she kissed me.

The rest was too much of a heavenly blur to be described in a coherent sequence.

I licked their tight pussies, I kissed them, I fucked them. I was sandwiched between tits. I didn't have enough fingers to touch everything I wanted to feel at once. My cock went from one to another while they kissed each other, kneading each other's breasts, rubbing each other's sensitive clits. I kissed and was kissed. I watched them eat each other. I swear, for a few minutes, I thought I'd died and gone to X-rated heaven. And then, just as Blondie was about to come, just as I was about to give her my all, Blue-Hair inserted a couple of fingers into her ass. I gushed into her as she yelped. I felt her wet pussy spasm onto my shaft and let out a groan, my heart matching the salsa rhythm still resonating below us.

But when my senses came back to me, they were accompanied by a long list of realizations:

Bright-blue hair, but a blonde landing strip. Two hot, beach-looking babes with full-body tans. Fingers in the ass just before coming.

Fuck.

Are these two the blonde lesbians I was looking for?

9:25 P.M.

I GOT out of bed and started dressing myself.

"May be a little late to ask, but I didn't catch your names earlier, with the loud music and all," I asked, bringing up my pants.

"I'm Isabel," Blue-Hair said.

"And I'm Tracy," Blondie said.

I pulled up my pants' zipper, snickering. "I can't fucking believe it."

"What?" Tracy asked with round eyes.

I shook my head. "I came to Cancun looking for the both of you. I was at your boat a few hours ago, but you weren't there. Obviously. Some older couple said I might be able to find you in this bar."

"What?" Tracy asked again. "Why were you looking for us?"

I let out a long sigh then began telling the tale of the mysterious diary that had come to be in my possession. Once I divulged what I knew of their encounter with the stewardess, large smiles appeared on their faces. Tracy moved to sit behind Isabel, then wrapped her arms around her waist.

"She wrote about us in her journal?" Isabel asked.

I nodded.

"Good things?" Tracy asked before gently kissing her girlfriend on the neck.

"Better than you could ever imagine," I replied. "Do you know her name?"

Isabel turned her head to look at Tracy. They stared at each other for a second, squinting. Isabel then turned to face me again. "Don't think we even asked... I was so pleased to have reeled in a hottie onto our boat for Tracy's birthday."

"So, that's what I am? Another prey that you reeled in for some celebration or another?" I asked, intrigued by their behavior.

"I guess you could see it that way... But didn't you have fun?"

"What are you celebrating?"

"Our one-year wedding anniversary," Isabel said before stealing a kiss from her wife.

I snickered again. "Congrats! Glad you opted to fuck me instead of buying each other flowers. But why didn't we just head back to your nice boat instead of this..."

"Dump?" Isabel finished.

I nodded, glad she'd said it and not me.

Both of them grinned. "Rocking the boat isn't good for our reputation," Isabel said. "We try to avoid it whenever we can."

"But that yacht. Aren't you rich? Can't you afford something a little less... dodgy?"

Isabel got up and walked up to me, her nipples still erect. Her hands buttoned up the shirt that I'd just picked up from the floor and donned. "It may surprise you," she started, "but there are many freaks out there. It's not like we do this every day or every week. But maybe once a month or so. We don't want the random men or women we hook up with to know that we're wealthy. We're not looking for anything serious, and we definitely don't want someone to start blackmailing us or start begging us for money. Coming here is safe. Nacho downstairs knows us, and he keeps things... private, if you know what I mean."

Isabel had finished doing up my shirt. She bent down to grab my tie, and I couldn't help but slap her beautiful ass.

"Hey!" she yelped with fake outrage.

"So, that flight attendant. You wouldn't happen to remember what airline she was with, would you?"

Tracy and Isabel looked at each other again, then shook their heads. "We fly with whichever airline has the most convenient flights for where we're going. Anything else you need to know?" Isabel asked, now doing up my tie for me.

"I have no idea what she even looks like. Any chance you have a picture?"

"Of her face? No," Isabel replied.

"But we have another you may want to see," Tracy said before rolling out of bed. She dug a phone out of the red pants that lay about a foot from her. She unlocked her device, then flicked her finger through several screens. I walked toward her.

While she was rummaging through her pictures, I asked Isabel about the sex tape they'd given the coastguard.

"That? He loved it," she said before pausing for a few seconds. "We saw him a few months later, and he asked if we had made a copy of it. Turns out that his wife found him masturbating to it in their bedroom one day, so she went at it with a hammer and destroyed it."

"And? Did you have a copy of it?"

Isabel shook her head.

"I found the photo!" Tracy exclaimed, bouncing to her feet, her perky, small breasts barely bouncing around. She moved the screen closer to me. I looked at the two naked women standing next to me and compared their tits with the selfie in front of me. The other two nipples were those of my mystery woman.

"Nice breasts, no?" Tracy asked rhetorically.

"All of you have gorgeous tits," I answered, handing Tracy back her phone then grabbing a breast from each of the naked women and giving them a good squeeze.

"Stop it," Isabel said, swatting my hand. I let go of their breasts to pick up my uniform jacket.

"How would you describe her?"

"Brunette, curvy, a bit taller than us I think," Isabel started. "She's beautiful but doesn't know it. A bit of a girl-next-door you could say? I wasn't sure if she'd be up for it, but believe me... she didn't disappoint."

Tracy let out a sigh. "Hell no!"

I ARRIVED at the airport an hour after leaving my gorgeous lesbians. I returned my rented convertible, and then got myself a seat on the red-eye flight to New York.

These two blonde beauties had taught me something: I had no idea lesbians could crave cocks from time to time... Interesting... Or maybe they're bi. Anyway, I was glad to have shared that experience with them, prey or not.

While waiting for my plane to board, I observed women strolling by, especially the stewardesses. One of them could be her. Just as the thought crossed my mind, a brunette walked by, her airline carry-on rolling behind her. Her high-heels and slender calves enticed my eyes to continue their upward scan of her body, albeit covered by her uniform. She was great looking, with a curvy hip-to-waist ratio, but her tits were B-cups at best.

Not my gal.

I didn't know what I expected my stewardess to look like physically, but I was glad to now know that she was an attractive, tall, curvy brunette with solid C-cup tits. I didn't have a preference in terms of ethnicity, but knowing that she was Caucasian certainly didn't simplify my quest.

Damn it! I should have asked the girls to forward me that wet T-shirt selfie. Well, I got distracted by those blonde lesbian beauties. That's okay, though. I think I've got her gorgeous tits and large nipples engrained in my head now.

Knowing these physical details about her will make my next reading of her Costa Rica entry a lot more lively. I'll be able to imagine my mysterious brunette on the surf board, then on the beach... Those glorious tits...

I gotta book myself some free time to fly down there so I can try to find her surf instructor. If I describe her to him— and mention what they did in his van and on the beach—he should remember my mysterious brunette.

He could even have her name written down on a surf lesson receipt...

TO BE CONTINUED...

...IN PART 3 of *The Stewardess's Diary*, available at most major book retailers.

The complete episodic novel is also available in one (thick) paperback with exclusive author's notes about the series and what inspired each episode.

ABOUT THE AUTHOR

S.M. Pratt is a single woman traveling the world on her own, living in the moment, looking for more than love, and always trying out new things. Fun adventures and unique cultural experiences are always at the top of her agenda, no matter the country she happens to be visiting.

She would love to quit her day job and write full-time. You can help her write the next story faster by purchasing her books and/or giving her five-star reviews. Without your support, she's invisible and unable to make a living doing what she loves, which is creating what you love to read.

If you haven't done so already, please join her private reader group for previews, exclusive offers, and more. It's free: https://smpratt.com

For more information:
smpratt.com
info@smpratt.com